Getting Started with the SAS® System

Version 8

SAS Institute Inc.
SAS Campus Drive
Cary, NC 27513

The correct bibliographic citation for this manual is as follows: SAS Institute Inc., *Getting Started with the SAS®
System, Version 8*, Cary, NC: SAS Institute Inc., 1999. 90 pp.

Getting Started with the SAS® System, Version 8

Copyright © 1999 by SAS Institute Inc., Cary, NC, USA.

ISBN 1-58025-579-5

SAS Institute Inc., SAS Campus Drive, Cary, North Carolina 27513.

1st printing, September 1999

SAS® and all other SAS Institute Inc. product or service names are registered trademarks or trademarks of SAS
Institute Inc. in the USA and other countries. ® indicates USA registration.

Other brand and product names are registered trademarks or trademarks of their respective companies.

The Institute is a private company devoted to the support and further development of its software and related services.

Table of Contents

Chapter 5 – Analyzing your data

Chapter 6 – Finding out more about SAS software

Welcome to the SAS System

Welcome to the SAS System, the industry leader in information delivery – the complete process of converting raw data, which organizations have in abundance, into the meaningful information that is required to support sucessful decision making. Knowledge is power, and data is *just data*. No matter how much data you have on hand, if you don't have a way to make sense of it, you really have nothing at all.

That's where the SAS System comes in.

The SAS System is an information delivery system that transforms data into information for better decision making. You can access and transform data from more than 50 different operational data stores, then manage and analyze your information and deliver it to any platform, in any format you need. It turns data – *any data* – into in-depth knowledge.

For example, with the SAS System you can

- read Oracle data on a mainframe computer and create a graphical report that can be viewed on a PC.

- read and analyze raw data on a UNIX server and create an HTML report. This report can be stored on a web server so that anyone in your organization can view it.

- submit a SAS program from your PC that reads and processes data on a mainframe computer, and then bring the output back to your PC for analysis.

Overview of SAS Software

Let's take a closer look at the SAS System. Its foundation gives you

- a powerful programming language
- ready-to-use procedures
- an easy-to-use windowing interface.

The SAS programming language enables you to access and manage your data. For example, you can read, transform, format, and combine data. You can also modify values and create variables.

Ready-To-Use Procedures let you analyze and present your data. For example, you can create tables and summary reports, and produce statistical analyses.

The SAS System is open and flexible, so you can add components to fit your needs. Components are available for

- data entry
- graphical reports
- advanced statistical and mathematical analysis
- business planning, forecasting and decision support
- operations research, project management, and quality improvement
- applications development.

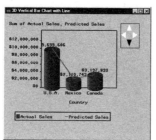

For specific industries, SAS also offers a variety of customized business solutions.

Easy-to-use interfaces help you see and manipulate your information. The SAS workspace enables you to write and edit SAS programs, as well as manage your data and output. You can add a point-and-click client application to quickly accomplish tasks such as generating sophisticated reports and queries. No matter which interface you use, the power of the SAS programming language is there to help you access, manage, analyze and present your data.

Whatever the industry, whatever the task, the SAS System turns data into knowledge.

Using this book

Getting Started with the SAS System is a tutorial designed to get you started using SAS software quickly and easily. You don't need any special knowledge to use this book – it's organized so that you can jump right in and start learning to use SAS software for basic data tasks. Step-by-step instructions and screen captures guide you through each task.

You can do all the tasks in order, or skip around and do only the tasks that interest you. Along the way, you'll gain a familiarity with features of SAS that will help you in any task you do later. If you decide to skip around, be sure to go through the tasks in Chapter 2 first. **Chapter 2 covers the basic tasks which serve as a foundation for the other tasks in this book.**

The chapters are organized with various high-level data tasks in mind:

Chapter 2 introduces the SAS workspace and gets you started with some basic tasks such as assigning a library for your files, creating a table, and performing basic file management tasks.

Chapter 3 covers the basics of accessing and managing data, such as browsing and editing tables, exporting and importing data and creating a query.

In **Chapter 4** you learn how to present your data by creating HTML output, a basic report, a tabular report and several types of drillable reports and graphs.

Chapter 5 covers basic data analyses such as summary statistics, simple regression analysis and surface plots.

Software requirements

To do all the tasks in this book, you must have the following software licensed:

- base SAS software
- SAS/EIS software
- SAS/GRAPH software
- SAS/STAT software
- SAS MDDB server.

The tasks in this book are also available in an online tutorial. To open the tutorial, select **Help ➤ Getting Started with SAS Software** from one of the main SAS windows.

Notes

Welcome to the SAS workspace

The SAS System is designed to be easy to use. It provides windows for accomplishing all the basic SAS tasks you need to do. Once you get familiar with the starting points for your SAS tasks, you are ready to accomplish any task that SAS software can do.

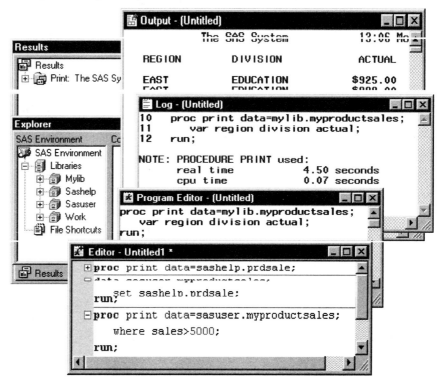

Touring SAS windows

When you first start SAS software, you see the five main SAS windows: the *Explorer*, *Results*, *Program Editor*, *Log*, and *Output* windows. In the Windows operating environment, the *Editor* window appears instead of the *Program Editor*.

This quick walkthrough shows you each of these windows and how they are used.

Tip
The arrangement of your SAS windows depends on your operating environment. Windows may overlay one another.

Explorer window

In the *Explorer* window, you can view and manage your SAS files, and create shortcuts to non-SAS files. Use this window to create new libraries and SAS files, to open any SAS file, and to perform most file management tasks such as moving, copying, and deleting files.

You can choose to display the *Explorer* window with or without a tree view of its contents.

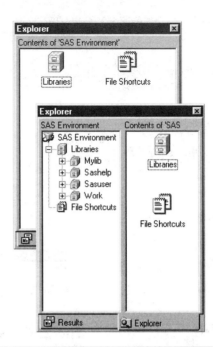

Program Editor window

In the *Program Editor* window, you enter, edit, and submit SAS programs. To open your SAS programs in desktop environments, you can drag and drop them onto the *Program Editor* window.

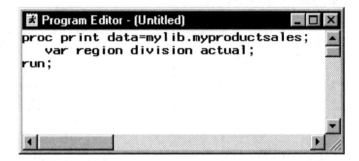

Enhanced Editor window

In the Windows operating environment, you use one or more *Editor* windows to enter, edit, and submit SAS programs. The *Editor* provides a number of useful editing features, including

- color coding and syntax checking of SAS language

- expandable and collapsible sections

- recordable macros

- support for keyboard shortcuts (Alt or Shift plus keystroke)

- multi-level undo and redo

and much more.

The initial *Editor* window title is Editor -Untitled*n* until you open a file or save the contents of the editor to a file. Then the window title changes to reflect that file name. When the contents of the editor are modified, an asterisk is added to the title.

Tip

If you prefer to use the *Program Editor* window, you can open it by selecting **View** ➔ **Program Editor**.

```
Editor - Untitled1 *
proc print data=sashelp.prdsale;
data sasuser.myproductsales;
    set sashelp.prdsale;
run;
proc print data=sasuser.myproductsales;
    where sales > 5000;
run;
```

Log window

The *Log* window displays messages about your SAS session and any SAS programs you submit.

Output window

In the *Output* window, you can browse output from SAS programs that you submit.

By default, the *Output* window is positioned behind the other windows. When you create output, the *Output* window automatically moves to the front of your display.

Results window

The *Results* window helps you navigate and manage output from SAS programs that you submit. You can view, save, and print individual items of output.

By default, the *Results* window is positioned behind the *Explorer* window and it is empty until you submit a SAS program that creates output. Then it moves to the front of your display.

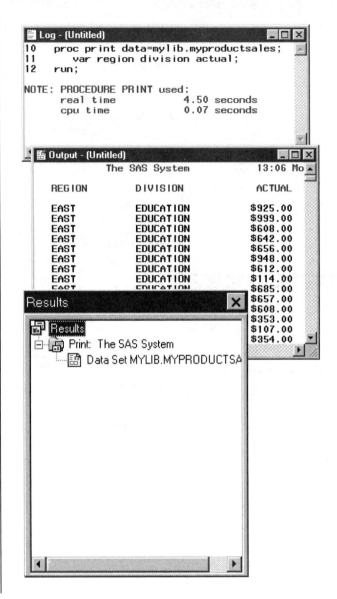

Using SAS window features

SAS windows have many features that help you get your work done. This quick walkthrough shows you how to manage your SAS windows, use menus and pop-up menus, use toolbars, and get more help.

Manage your SAS windows

In the Windows operating environment, you can send windows that you aren't using to the SAS window bar.

❶ On the *Editor* window, click the Minimize button to send it to the SAS window bar.

❷ Click Editor on the SAS window bar to restore the window to its former position.

Use menus

Each window in the workspace has its own menu selections that reflect the actions you can perform in the window.

❶ Click the *Explorer* window.

❷ Select the **View** menu, which lists options to change how your icons or files are displayed in the *Explorer* window.

❸ Click the *Editor* (or in some operating environments, the *Program Editor* window). Select the **View** menu and notice that it offers different selections.

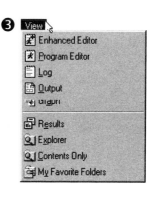

Use pop-up menus

❶ In the *Explorer* window, right-click the Libraries icon. Notice that **Open** and **New** are available in the pop-up menu. Select **Open**.

❷ Right-click the Sasuser icon. The pop-up menu contains additional selections. Click anywhere outside the pop-up menu to close it without selecting an action.

❸ Select **View ➡ Up One Level** to return to the top level of the *Explorer* window.

Use toolbar tools

The toolbar displays icons for many of the actions you perform most often in a particular window.

❶ Click the *Explorer* window and look at the toolbar. Notice that currently unavailable tools are grayed.

❷ Move your mouse pointer to a tool and hold it there for a moment. A Screen Tip displays the name of the tool.

❸ Click the *Editor* (or *Program Editor*) window and view the tools available.

❶
Open
New...

❷
Open
Explore From Here
New...
Delete
Properties

❶
❷ Toggle Tree

❸

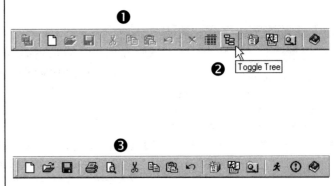

Getting more help

Help is available for all products in the SAS System. You can access different kinds of help from the Help menu. You can get help for all SAS software products or you can get task-oriented help for one window at a time. Reference documentation is now available on CD-ROM and can also be accessed from the Help menu.

Open SAS System help

❶ Select **Help ➡ SAS System**.

❷ Select topics from the Contents list in the left pane of the window and read the help in the right pane of the window.

Open Using This Window help

❶ Click the *Explorer* window to make it active.

❷ Select **Help ➡ Using This Window** or click the Help tool on the toolbar.

❸ Task-oriented help for using the *Explorer* window appears. This type of help is available from all the main SAS windows.

Open SAS OnlineDoc

❶ Select **Help ➡ Books and Training ➡ SAS OnlineDoc**.

❷ Select topics from the Contents list in the left pane of the window and read the documentation in the right pane of the window.

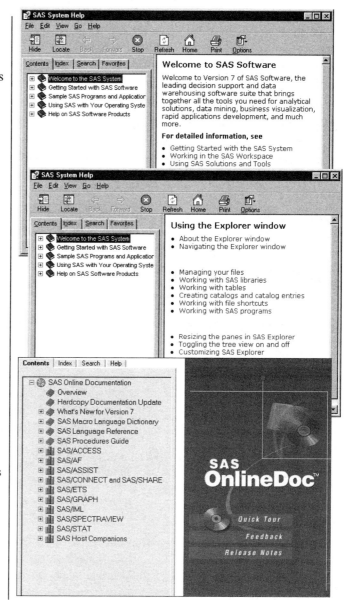

Exploring files

In SAS software, you can use windows to explore and manage both SAS files and other files. This quick walkthrough shows you how to explore files in SAS libraries using the *Explorer* window, and explore files in your operating environment using the *My Favorite Folders* window.

Tip

You can also move up through open folders by selecting **View ➧ Up One Level** or by pressing the Backspace key.

Tip

All files are displayed in the *My Favorite Folders* window, but only registered file types have actions associated with them. You can delete, rename, copy, and move files using this window.

Explore files in SAS libraries

In the *Explorer* window, you can view and manage your SAS files, which are stored in libraries. You can think of the library name as a temporary nickname or shortcut for the physical location of the files (such as a directory).

❶ In the *Explorer* window, double-click Libraries. The active libraries are listed.

❷ Double-click the Sashelp library. All members of the Sashelp library are listed.

❸ Move back up to the top level of the *Explorer* window by clicking twice on the Up One Level tool on the toolbar.

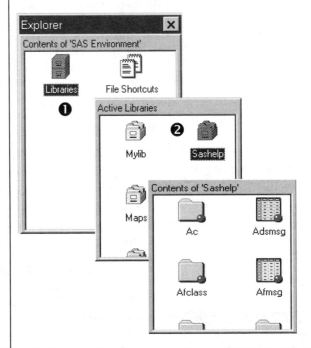

Explore files in your operating environment

❶ Select **View ➧ My Favorite Folders**.

❷ Open folders and browse your files.

❸ When you are finished, select **File ➧ Close** to close the *My Favorite Folders* window.

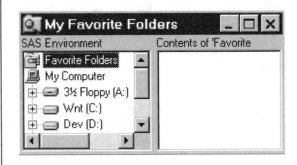

Working with SAS files

The *Explorer* window makes it easy to manage your SAS files. This quick walkthrough shows you how to view details about files, sort files in libraries, view file properties, and open a file. In this example you work with the Prdsale table, which contains product sales data.

View details about files

You can view a library's contents as large icons, as small icons, as a list, or with details displayed.

❶ Open the Sashelp library.

❷ Click the Details tool. Information about the files is displayed.

❸ Resize the Details columns by moving the pointer over the separator bar between the detail fields. When the pointer changes to a resizing tool, click and drag the separator bar to get the desired size.

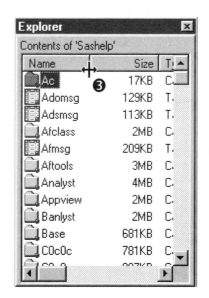

Sort files

Files in the *Explorer* window are sorted alphabetically by file name. You can sort by any column in ascending or descending order.

❶ Click the Type column to sort the files by file type.

❷ Click the Type column again to reverse the sort order.

❸ Select **View ➧ Refresh** to return the files to their original order.

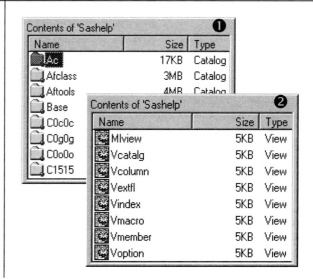

Working with SAS files

Tip
To open the *Properties* window with Columns selected, right-click a table and select **View Columns**.

Note
Properties that can be modified have a **Modify** pop-up menu item. You cannot modify all the properties of a file, and you cannot modify the properties of items in the Sashelp library.

View file properties

❶ In the Sashelp library, right-click the Prdsale table and select **Properties** from the pop-up menu. The *Properties* window opens with General Properties displayed.

❷ Click the drop-down arrow at the top of the window to look at other property categories. Select Columns to view column properties.

❸ Click OK to close the *Properties* window.

Open a file
You can view the contents of SAS files directly from the *Explorer* window.

❶ Double-click the Prdsale table to open it. The table opens in the *VIEWTABLE* window in browse mode.

❷ When you are finished looking at the data in the table, select **File → Close** from the *VIEWTABLE* window.

❸ Return to the top level of the *Explorer* window.

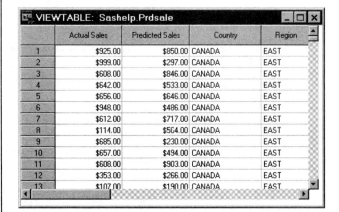

Working with SAS libraries

SAS files, such as tables and catalogs, are stored in **libraries**. By default, SAS software defines several libraries for you (including Sashelp, Sasuser, and Work).

When you define a library, you indicate the location of your SAS files to SAS software. When you delete a SAS library, the pointer is deleted, and SAS software no longer has access to the directory. However, the contents of the library still exist in your operating environment.

Once you create a library, you can manage SAS files within it. This quick walkthrough shows you how to assign a new library, copy a table into your new library, and rename the table.

Tip

Take a look at the engines available for creating libraries. Depending on your operating environment, you can create libraries using engines that allow you to read different file formats, including file formats from other vendors.

Assign a new library

❶ In the *Explorer* window, double-click Libraries.

❷ In Active Libraries, select **File ➤ New...**

❸ In the *New Library* window, type Mylib for the name, and leave the Default engine selected. An engine is a set of internal instructions SAS software uses for writing to and reading from files in a library..

❹ Select Enable at startup so that the library is created each time you start SAS.

❺ Click Browse and select a directory to use for this library. In the Select dialog you must open the directory you want to use so that the full path into that directory is assigned. Click OK.

❻ Click OK to assign the library. Mylib appears in the Active Libraries list.

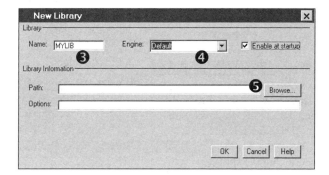

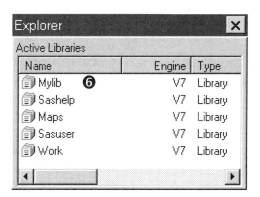

Copy a table

❶ With the *Explorer* window active, select **View ➥ Show Tree**. The *Explorer* window now contains two panes.

❷ In the left pane, single-click the Sashelp library to show the library's contents in the right pane. Scroll to the icon for the Prdsale table.

❸ Click the Prdsale table. To copy the table to your Mylib library, drag and drop it on Mylib in the left pane. Notice the message in the message bar.

❹ Open Mylib and confirm that the table was copied.

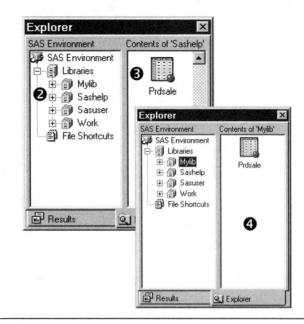

Rename the table

❶ In the Mylib library, right-click the Prdsale table and select Rename from the pop-up menu.

❷ Type `MyProductSales` and click OK.

❸ In the left pane of the *Explorer* window, click SAS Environment to return to the top level. Select **View ➥ Show Tree** to toggle off the tree view.

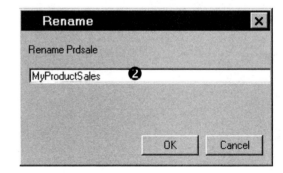

Working with SAS programs

SAS programs can serve many purposes. Some merely open windows that enable you to accomplish your task. You can write others that are complex enough to meet any of the data processing needs of your organization. All SAS programs can produce results with a few powerful statements. This quick walkthrough shows you how to create and save a SAS program, submit the program, and view and save your results.

Create and save a program

❶ In the top level of the *Explorer* window, select **File ➠ New**.

❷ Select Source Program, and click OK.

❸ Type the following program into the *NOTEPAD* window:

```
proc print
data=mylib.myproductsales;
run;
```

This program prints a listing of the MyProductSales table that you stored in your Mylib library.

❹ Select **File ➠ Save As**. Leave the default directory selected and type `myprog.sas` in the File name box. Click OK or Save.

Submit the program

❶ Click the *NOTEPAD* window to activate it. If the window isn't visible, click the Notepad button in the SAS window bar.

❷ Select **Run ➠ Submit**. The *Output* and *Results* windows come to the front.

Working with SAS programs

View and save results

You can view, save, and manage individual results in the *Results* window.

❶ In the *Results* window, click the expansion icon (+) beside the Results node to open it if necessary. Click the expansion icon (+) to open the folder for the Print procedure output.

❷ Double-click Data Set MYLIB.MYPRODUCTSALES. The *Output* window scrolls to the top of the Print procedure output.

❸ Click Data Set MYLIB.MYPRODUCTSALES and select Save As Object from the pop-up menu. In the Save As dialog, the output is saved by default as Sasuser.Profile.Print. Click Save.

❹ Click the Programming Windows tool to restore the windows to their default position.

Note
In the Windows and OS/2 operating environments, the Programming Windows tool restores the main windows to their default position and also opens the *Program Editor* window. If you prefer to use the *Editor* window, you can restore it from the SAS window bar.

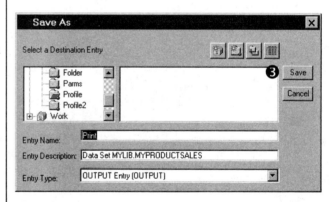

Using file shortcuts

You can create a file shortcut to any type of file. Instead of having to locate your SAS programs stored in various places on your host system, you can create file shortcuts to the programs you use often. The shortcuts are stored in the File Shortcuts folder in the Explorer window. This quick walkthrough shows you how to create a file shortcut and open a file using the shortcut.

Note

If you have used SAS before, you may be familiar with the term "file reference" or "fileref". A file shortcut is the same as a file reference or fileref.

Create a file shortcut

In this example, you create a shortcut to the SAS program you created earlier.

❶ In the top level of the *Explorer* window, double-click the File Shortcuts icon.

❷ Select **File ➤ New**.

❸ Type `PrintNew` as the file shortcut name. Click Browse and select the myprog.sas program you created. Click Open or OK.

❹ Click OK. File Shortcuts now contains your Printnew file shortcut.

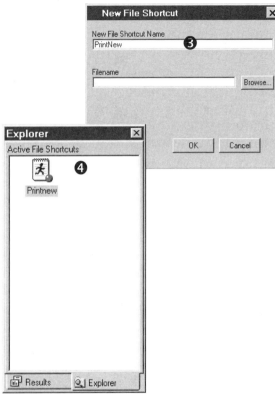

Using file shortcuts

Open and submit the file shortcut

❶ Double-click the Printnew file shortcut. The program opens in the *Editor* (or *Program Editor*) window.

❷ Click the Submit tool on the toolbar to run the program.

❸ In the *Results* window, open the folder for the second Print procedure.

❹ Double-click Data Set MYLIB.MYPRODUCTSALES to scroll to the top of the Print procedure output.

❺ In the *Results* window, right-click the top folder labeled Print: The SAS System. Select Delete from the popup menu.

❻ In the Delete Confirmation box, click Yes. The pointer for the first print procedure is deleted and that part of the output in the *Output* window is also deleted.

❼ Click the Programming Windows tool on the toolbar to restore windows to their default positions. Close the *Notepad* window and return to the top level of the *Explorer* window.

Tip

A convenient way to assign a file shortcut is to select **View ➡ My Favorite Folders**, find the SAS program file you want, and select Create File Shortcut from the pop-up menu.

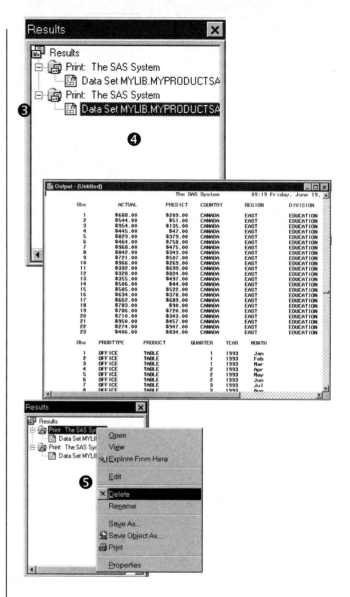

Accessing and Managing your Data

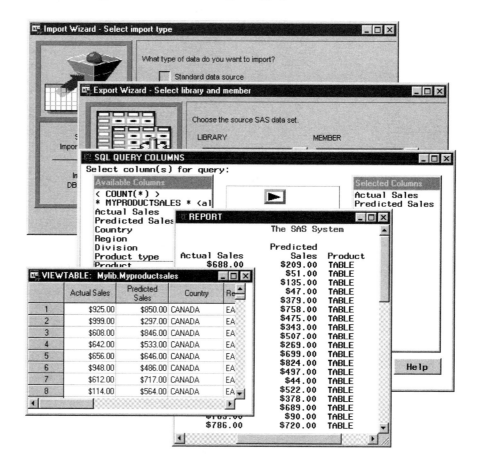

Browsing and editing data

To manipulate data interactively, you can use SAS software's table editor, the *VIEWTABLE* window. This quick walkthrough shows you how to browse a table, move and label columns, and edit cell values.

Open an existing table

In the *VIEWTABLE* window, you can create a new table, or you can edit or browse an existing table. In the example below, you work with the table Mylib.MyProductSales, which contains sample data for product sales.

❶ Select **Tools ➤ Table Editor** to open the *VIEWTABLE* window.

❷ Select **File ➤ Open**. The Open dialog displays the current SAS libraries.

❸ Under Libraries, select Mylib. The tables and views in the Mylib library are displayed on the right.

❹ Double-click MyProductSales. The *VIEWTABLE* window opens. Scroll the *VIEWTABLE* window to view Mylib.MyProductSales.

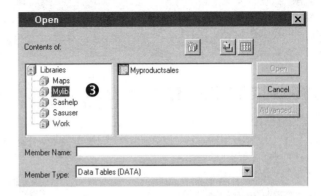

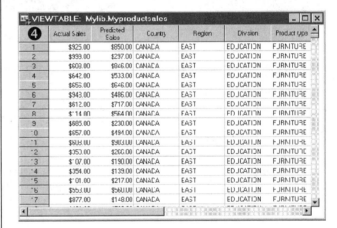

Move and label columns

Within the *VIEWTABLE* window, you can rearrange columns and temporarily change column headings.

❶ Single-click the heading for Country. Then drag and drop Country onto Actual Sales. The Country column moves to the right of the Actual Sales column.

❷ Right-click the heading for Region and select Column Attributes from the pop-up menu.

❸ In the Label box, type `Sales Region` and then click Apply.

❹ Click Close.

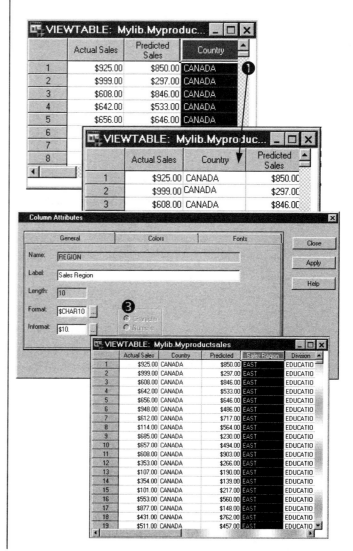

Sort by values of a column

You can sort your table in ascending or descending order, based on the values of a column. You can sort data permanently or create a sorted copy of your table. In this example, you create a sorted copy.

❶ Right-click the heading for Product and select Sort from the pop-up menu.

❷ Select Descending.

❸ When the warning message appears, click Yes to create a sorted copy of the table.

❹ In the *Sort* window, type `Mylib.Mysorted` as the name for the sorted table. Then click OK. Rows in the new table are sorted in descending order by values of Product.

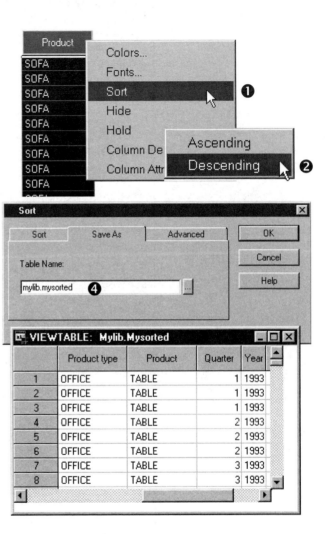

Edit cell values

By default, *VIEWTABLE* opens existing tables in browse mode, which protects the table data. To edit the table, you need to switch to edit mode.

❶ Select **Edit → Edit Mode**.

❷ Click the first cell in the Country column. Highlight the existing value and type GERMANY. Then press Enter. The value in the cell is updated.

❸ Select **File → Close**. When prompted about saving changes to the table, click No. (You don't want to save the edit you made.)

	Actual Sales	Country	Predicted Sales
1	$688.00	GERMANY ❷	$209.00
2	$544.00	CANADA	$51.00
3	$954.00	CANADA	$135.00
4	$445.00	CANADA	$47.00
5	$829.00	CANADA	$379.00
6	$464.00	CANADA	$758.00
7	$968.00	CANADA	$475.00
8	$842.00	CANADA	$343.00
9	$721.00	CANADA	$507.00

VIEWTABLE: Mylib.Myproductsales

Exporting a subset of your data

As you work with tables in the *VIEWTABLE* window, you can export all or part of the data using SAS software's Export Wizard. This quick walkthrough shows you how to browse a table, subset rows, export data, and clear subsets.

Subset rows of a table

In the *VIEWTABLE* window, you can subset the display to show only those rows that meet one or more conditions.

❶ In the *Explorer* window, open the Mylib library. Double-click MyProductSales. The *VIEWTABLE* window displays Mylib.MyProductSales.

❷ Right-click any table cell (not a heading) and select Where from the pop-up menu. The *WHERE EXPRESSION* window opens.

❸ In the Available Columns list, select REGION. From the pop-up menu, select EQ (equal to).

❹ In the Available Columns list, select <LOOKUP distinct values>. In the *Lookup Values* window, select WEST.

Notice that the complete Where expression appears in the Where box.

❺ Click OK. The *VIEWTABLE* window now displays only rows where the value of Region is WEST.

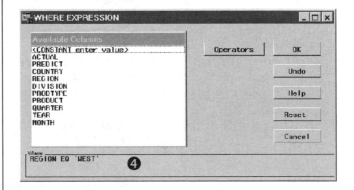

Exporting a subset of your data

Export data

You can easily export SAS data to a variety of file formats. The formats that are available depend on your operating environment and the SAS software products you have installed.

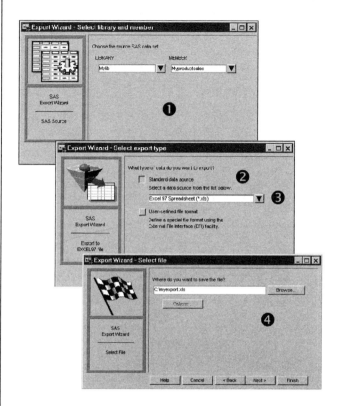

❶ Select **File ➤ Export Data**. The *Export Wizard* window opens. Note that the LIBRARY and MEMBER lists contain the name of the table (Mylib.MyProductSales) currently displayed in the *VIEWTABLE* window.

❷ Click Next to proceed to selecting an export type. Notice that Standard data source is selected by default.

❸ In the data source list, select Excel 97 Spreadsheet (*.xls) or another format available on your operating environment.

❹ Click Next to proceed to selecting a destination file. Click Browse and select a directory. Type the file name `myexport` and click OK.

❺ Click Finish. The SAS table is exported to Myexport in the directory you selected.

Note

To select Excel 97 Spreadsheet (*.xls), you must have SAS/ACCESS PC File Formats software installed. Otherwise, you can select Tab Delimited File (*.txt).

Exporting a subset of your data

Clear subsets

If you have subset rows in the *VIEWTABLE* window, you can clear subsets and then redisplay all data in the table.

❶ Right-click anywhere in the table except a column heading.

❷ Select Where Clear from the pop-up menu. The *VIEWTABLE* window removes any existing subset(s) and displays all rows in the table.

❸ Select **File → Close**.

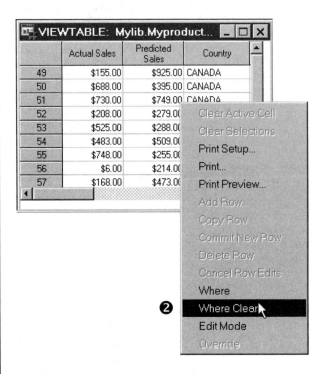

Importing data into a table

Whether your data are stored in a standard file format or in your own special file format, SAS software's Import Wizard can guide you through the steps of importing data into a SAS table. This quick walkthrough shows you how to import a standard file and view the results.

Note

The types of files that can be imported depend on your operating system.

Tip

If your data are not in a standard file format, you can use the External File Interface (EFI) facility to import data. This tool enables you to define your file format and offers you a range of format options. To use the EFI, simply select User-defined file format in the *Import Wizard* and follow directions for describing your data file.

Import a standard file

❶ Select **File → Import Data** to open the *Import Wizard*. Notice that Standard data source is selected by default.

❷ Click the drop-down arrow for the list of data sources. If you exported data to Excel, select Excel 97 Spreadsheet (*.xls). Otherwise, select the file format in which your data are stored.

❸ Click Next to continue. In the *Import Wizard - Select file* window, type the full path for your file or click Browse to find it.

❹ Click Next to continue. In the *Import Wizard - Select library and member* window, type Mylib for the library name and MyImport for the member name.

❺ Click Next to continue. If you are importing data from the Excel 97 Spreadsheet format, you are asked about saving PROC IMPORT statements. Skip this option and click Finish. Your data are imported into the SAS table Mylib.MyImport.

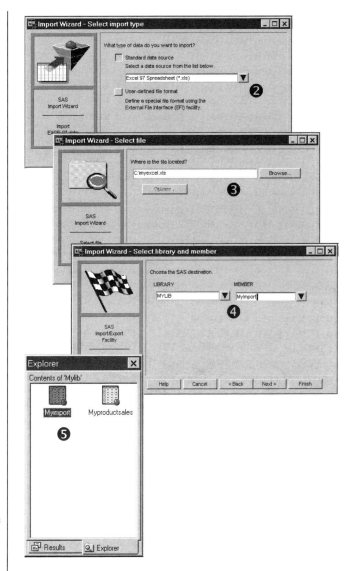

Creating a query

Sometimes you need quick answers to questions about your data. To perform simple and complex queries (including joins) interactively, you can use SAS software's *SQL Query* window. This quick walkthrough shows you how to select data, subset rows, create a column, and view the results of your query and the SQL statements in the query.

Tip

To join tables, right-click anywhere in the *SQL QUERY COLUMNS* window and select Tables from the pop-up menu. Then repeat steps 2-4 for each remaining table that you want to join.

Select data for the query

As input to your query, you can select 32 tables and any number of columns.

❶ Select **Tools ➡ Query**.

❷ In the Table Sources list, select MYLIB. Then double-click MYLIB.MYPRODUCTSALES in the Available Tables list to move it to the Selected Tables list.

❸ Click OK. *The SQL QUERY COLUMNS* window appears.

❹ In the Available Columns list, double-click Actual Sales, Predicted Sales, and Product, in turn. Now three columns appear in the Selected Columns list.

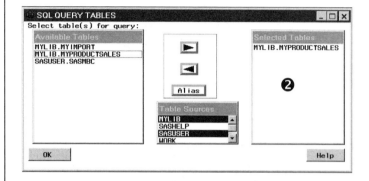

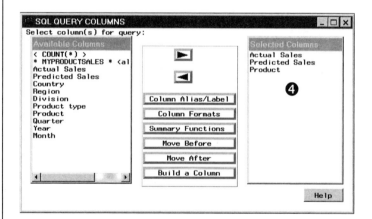

Subset rows

You can subset rows in your query based on one or more conditions. In the example below you select only rows for the eastern sales region.

❶ Right-click anywhere in the *SQL QUERY COLUMNS* window and select Where Conditions for Subset from the pop-up menu. The *WHERE EXPRESSION* window appears.

❷ In the Available Columns list, select Region. From the pop-up menu, select EQ (equal to).

❸ At the bottom of the Available Columns list, select <LOOKUP distinct values>. In the *Lookup Distinct Values* window, select EAST.

❹ The WHERE expression in the Where box is Region EQ 'EAST'. Click OK.

When joining tables, be sure to specify a WHERE condition that provides criteria for matching rows. For example, to match ID numbers in table A and table B, specify the WHERE condition a.idnum=b.idnum. Otherwise, you may create a tremendous amount of output.

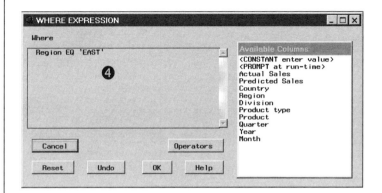

Creating a query

Create a new column

You can calculate new columns for your query. In the example below, you create the column Bonus as a percentage of actual sales.

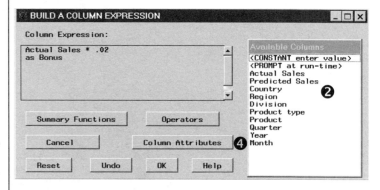

❶ In the *SQL QUERY COLUMNS* window, click Build a Column. The *BUILD A COLUMN EXPRESSION* window opens.

❷ In the Available Columns list, select Actual Sales. In the pop-up menu, select * for multiplication.

❸ In the Available Columns list, select <CONSTANT enter value>. Type .02 and click OK.

❹ Click the Column Attributes button. In the *Expression Column Attributes* window, type Bonus in the Alias Name box. Click OK.

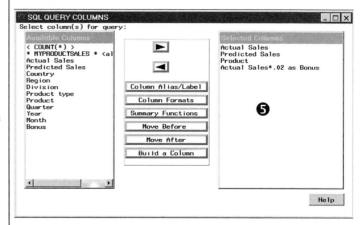

❺ In the *BUILD A COLUMN EXPRESSION* window, click OK. The new column appears in the Selected Columns list of the *SQL QUERY COLUMNS* window.

View results and query syntax

As you create your query, you can view your results and the SQL statements that the *SQL Query* window generates.

❶ Right-click anywhere in the *SQL QUERY COLUMNS* window and select Run Query. From the next pop-up menu, select Design a Report and then Begin with Default Report.

❷ In the *REPORT* window, view your output. Optionally, you can edit and save the report. Select **File ➜ Close**. When you are prompted about whether you are sure you want to leave the report, click OK.

❸ From the pop-up menu in the *SQL QUERY COLUMNS* window, select Show Query.

❹ The *SQL QUERY* window displays the SQL statements. Click Goback.

❺ Select **File ➜ Close**. When prompted about exiting the Query window environment, click OK.

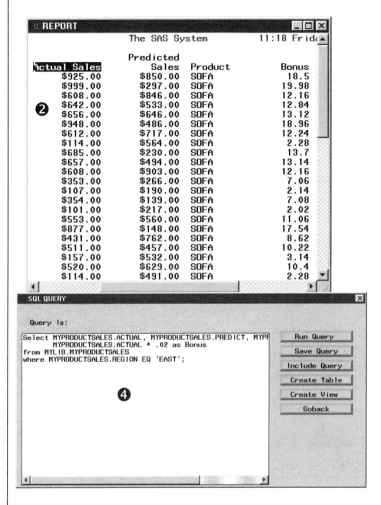

Notes

Presenting your data

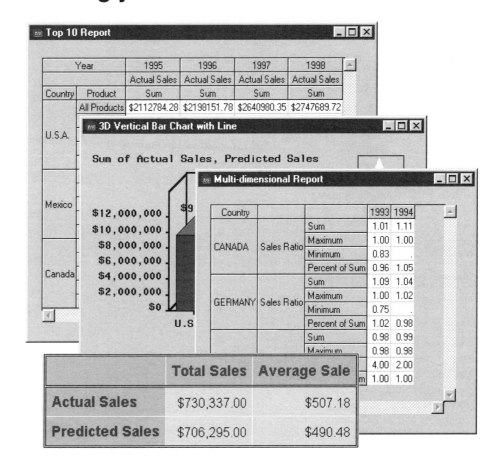

Creating HTML output

In Working with SAS Programs (Chapter 2), you submitted a SAS program and viewed your results in the *Output* window. The *Output* window displays listing output, which is traditional SAS output.

In desktop operating environments, you can also set preferences to create HTML output. You view SAS HTML output in your preferred browser. This quick walkthrough shows you how to specify HTML output and view and save your results.

Tip

You can create HTML output in any operating environment by using SAS programming statements.

Note

Specifying HTML output in your SAS preferences does not affect all SAS output. Some SAS tools (such as the Report Editor) create output in specialized windows. Others (such as the Analyst Application) enable you to control the format for only the output that they produce.

Specify HTML output

In desktop operating environments, you can specify HTML output in the Results tab of the *Preferences* window.

❶ From any SAS window, select **Tools ➡ Options ➡ Preferences**.

❷ In the *Preferences* window, click the Results tab. The options in this tab may vary depending on your operating environment.

❸ Select Create Listing, Create HTML, and Use WORK folder. These settings request both listing and HTML output, and specify that your HTML output be stored in your temporary WORK folder.

❹ If you are working in the Windows operating environment, choose a browser in the View results using box. The internal browser displays HTML output in the *Results Viewer* window.

❺ Click OK.

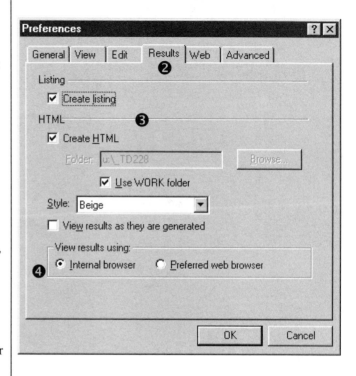

Submit a program

In this example, you submit the SAS program myprog.sas, which you saved in Working with SAS Programs (Chapter 2). The program prints the contents of a SAS data set.

❶ From the *Editor* or *Program Editor* window, select **File ➡ Open**.

❷ Select myprog.sas from the directory where you stored it previously. Then click Open or OK.

❸ Select **Run ➡ Submit**. The *Output* and *Results* windows come to the front.

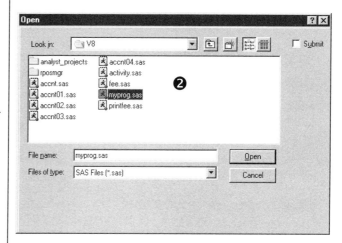

Creating HTML output

View and save your results

You can view, save, and manage both listing output and HTML output in the *Results* window.

❶ In the *Results* window, click the expansion icons (+) to open the Results node and the folder for the Print procedure output. Notice that different icons represent listing and HTML output.

❷ Double-click the icon for the second (HTML) output. If you selected Internal browser in the Windows operating environment, the HTML output appears in the *Results Viewer* window. Otherwise, the HTML output appears in your preferred browser.

❸ To save the contents of the *Results Viewer* window, select **File ➡ Save as**. In the *Save HTML Document* window, specify a file name and click Save.

To save the contents of your browser, select the equivalent browser menu items (typically **File Save As**) and specify a file name.

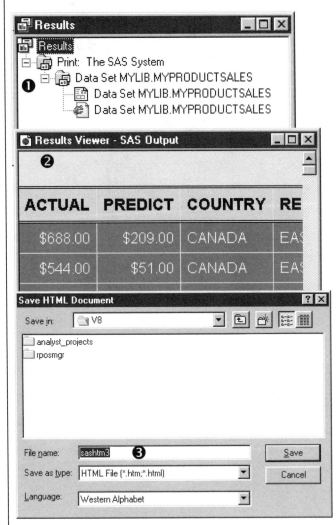

Creating a basic report

To create a variety of custom, presentation-quality reports, you can use SAS software's report editor, the *REPORT* window. This quick walkthrough shows you how to create and save a default report, select and order columns and rows, define columns, and display subtotals.

Create and save a default report

When you use the SAS report editor, you begin by creating a default listing of a SAS data set. Once you create the default report, you can modify the layout, structure, and appearance of the report.

❶ Select **Tools ➤ Report Editor**.

❷ In the Libraries list, select MYLIB. In the Datasets list, select MYPRODUCTSALES and click OK.

❸ The *REPORT* window displays the default report. (If your *REPORT* window is not wide enough to display all variables, the *MESSAGES* window indicates the number of variables displayed. Click OK.). Select **View ➤ Next Page** to scroll forward in the report.

❹ To save the report, select **File ➤ Save Report**. For Libname, Catalog, and Report name, type `sasuser`, `profile`, and `myrpt`, respectively. Optionally, type a description. Then click OK. The report definition is stored as Sasuser.Profile.Myrpt.Rept.

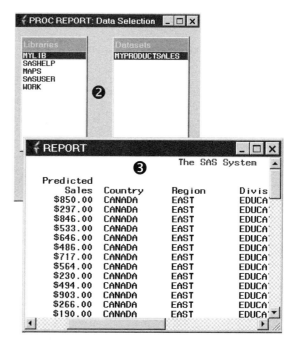

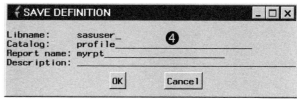

Delete, move, and define columns

❶ Click the header for Country. Then select **Edit ➡ Delete**. The column no longer appears in your report. Repeat the process for the columns Year and Month, if they appear in your report.

❷ Single-click the header for Quarter. Select **Edit ➡ Move ➡ Left of the Next Selected Item** and single-click the header for Actual Sales. Quarter moves to the left of Actual Sales.

❸ To define a column to group values, double-click the header for Quarter. Under Usage, select GROUP. Change the Header text from Quarter to Qtr.

❹ Click OK. The *REPORT* window displays values grouped by quarter. Notice that other columns formerly defined as DISPLAY columns (such as Region and Division) are now defined as GROUP columns along with Quarter. Values of Actual Sales are summed for each group.

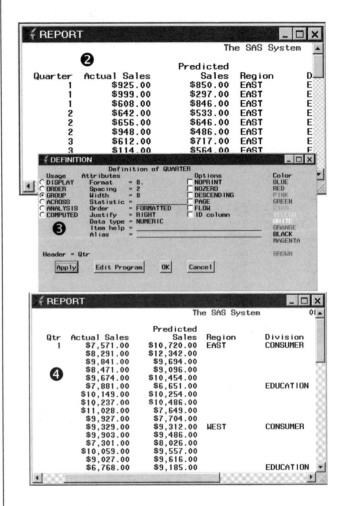

Sort and subset rows

You can order data in a report by defining one or more columns as order variables. Your report then sorts rows by the order variable values, displaying each unique order variable value only once. To show only rows that meet a certain condition or set of conditions, you can also subset the report.

❶ In the *REPORT* window, double-click the header for Division. Under Usage, select ORDER.

❷ Click OK. The *REPORT* window displays the revised report sorted by Division.

❸ Select **Subset ➠ Where**. In the *Where* window, type `product="SOFA"` to select only rows where the value of Product is SOFA. (The Where clause is case-sensitive, so be sure to type `SOFA` exactly as shown.)

❹ Click OK. The *REPORT* window displays only the rows you selected.

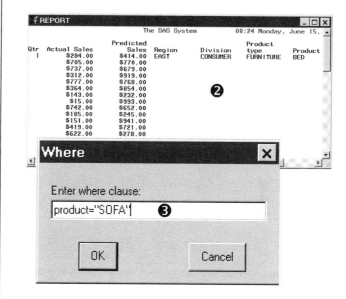

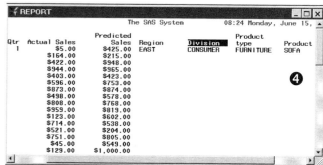

Display subtotals

You can insert subtotals in your report before or after items, and you can display totals at the top or bottom of the report.

❶ In the *REPORT* window, double-click the header for Quarter (Qtr). Under Usage, select GROUP.

❷ Click OK. The *REPORT* window displays the revised report grouped by quarter.

❸ With Qtr still selected, select **Edit ➡ Summarize Information ➡ After Item**. Under Options, select Overline summary, Skip line after break, and Summarize analysis columns. Under Color, select BLUE.

❹ Click OK. The revised report displays overlined subtotals for sales by quarter in blue.

❺ Close the *REPORT* window.

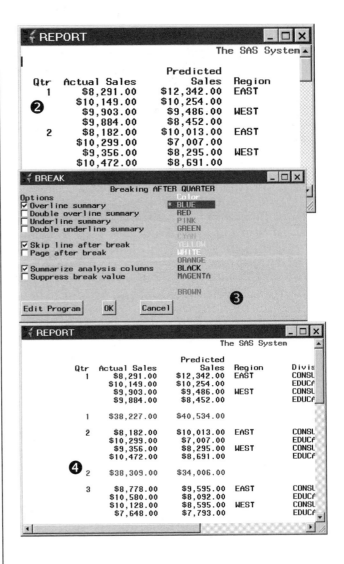

Creating a tabular report

To create tabular reports in any of a variety of layouts, you can use the Analyst Application. This quick walkthrough shows you how to select a table style, specify data and statistics, set report options, and view output and code for your report.

Tip

You can also choose to display source code as an item in the results tree.

Open a table and set preferences

To begin a report in the Analyst Application, you open an existing table or enter data in the data table provided. In the example below, you open the MyProductSales table that you created earlier.

❶ Select **Solutions ➡ Analysis ➡ Analyst**.

❷ Select **File ➡ Open By SAS Name**. In the Library list, select Mylib. Then select Myproductsales. Click OK. The MyProductSales data appear in the table, and a node for the MyProductSales data is added under New Project.

❸ Select **Tools ➡ Viewer Settings**. Click the Output tab. Clear the Provide source code checkbox and select the Create HTML file of results checkbox. Then click OK.

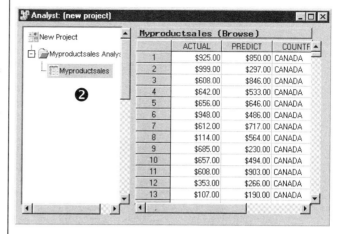

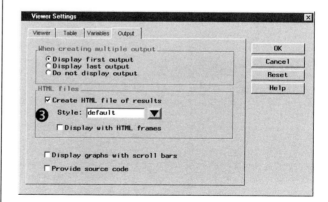

Creating a tabular report

Select a report style, variables, and statistics

For your tabular report, you select a table layout, variables, and statistics.

❶ Select **Reports ➨ Tables**. Then click the top left sample table. The *First Report Style: Myproductsales* window opens.

❷ In the list in the Statistics tab, double-click SUM and MEAN.

❸ Click the Analysis Variables tab.

❹ Double-click ACTUAL and PREDICT.

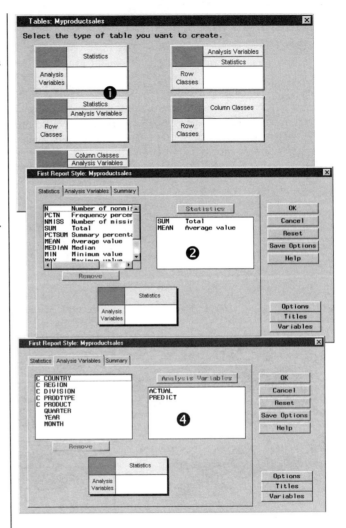

Set report options

You can set a number of options for your tabular report. In the example below, you specify a format for data values and labels for statistics.

❶ In the *First Report Style: Myproductsales* window, click Options.

❷ In the General tab, click the Default cell format arrow.

❸ In the Format Names list, select dollar. In the Decimal box, type 2. Click OK.

❹ Click the Labels tab. In the SUM box, type Total Sales. In the MEAN box, type Average Sale. Click OK.

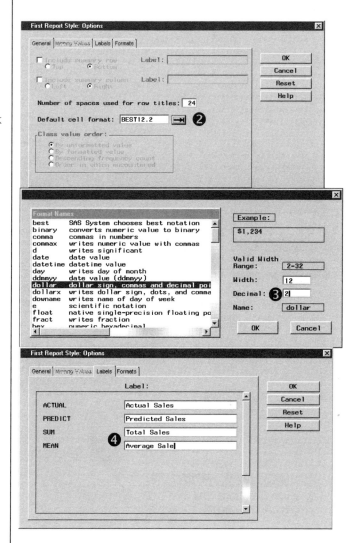

Creating a tabular report

View output

❶ In the *First Report Style: Myproductsales* window, click OK to run your report. Two versions of your report are generated: HTML output and standard output.

❷ View the HTML output in the *Results Viewer* window or your browser.

❸ Activate the *Analyst* window. Notice that a First Report Style node has been added to the project, with the items HTML and Report on Myproductsales.

❹ Double-click the Report on Myproductsales item and view the output. Then select **File ➡ Close**.

❺ In the *Analyst* window, select **File ➡ Close**. In the message dialog, click Do Not Save.

Note
Your tabular report and the SAS code for the report are presented in separate windows and organized in a tree list in the *Analyst* window.

Tip
You can save your entire project for later use.

❷	Total Sales	Average Sale
Actual Sales	$730,337.00	$507.18
Predicted Sales	$706,295.00	$490.48

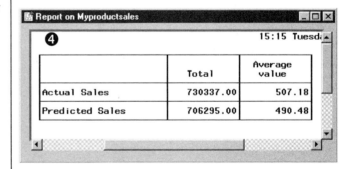

Report on Myproductsales   15:15 Tuesd

	Total	Average value
Actual Sales	730337.00	507.18
Predicted Sales	706295.00	490.48

Creating a drillable tabular report

To quickly create interactive, drillable reports, you can use report templates in the EIS / OLAP Report Gallery. This quick walkthrough shows you how to create and navigate a report, change the report layout, subset by dimension, calculate subtotal , and save the report as an Excel spreadsheet.

Add a table and create a basic report

❶ Select **Solutions** ➡ **Reporting** ➡ **EIS / OLAP Report Gallery**. Then double-click Tabular Reports.

❷ In the *Gallery of Tabular reports* window, open the pop-up menu and select Add Item. Then select Table. Select SASHELP in the Library list and PRDSAL2 in the Table list. Click OK. The PRDSAL2 table icon now appears in the window.

❸ Drag the PRDSAL2 icon and drop it on Top 10 Report. In the message window click Yes.

❹ In the *Column Selection* window, Down Dimensions is selected by default under Type. In the Available list, double-click Geographic to move it to the Selected list.

❺ In the Type column, click Analysis Variables. In the Available list, double-click Actual Sales to move it to the Selected list.

❻ Click OK. The report displays values of Country as rows, and Actual Sales and the statistic Sum as a column.

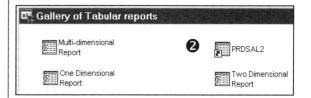

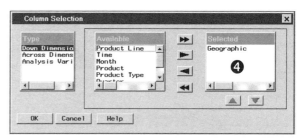

Navigate the table

❶ Click Canada and select Expand from the pop-up menu. Now sales are shown by province.

❷ Click Canada and select Collapse from the pop-up menu.

❸ To view Canadian sales only, double-click Canada. Now the report displays rows for State/Province, with the heading Subset: COUNTRY=Canada.

❹ To view sales in Quebec only, double-click Quebec. Now the report displays actual sales for Quebec, and the heading describes the new subset of data.

❺ To return to the previous level, click County and select Up from the pop-up menu. To continue navigating up, click State/Province and select Up from the pop-up menu.

❻ To show detail data for Canadian sales only, click Canada and select Show Detail Data from the pop-up menu. All values of Country are Canada. Select **File ➡ Close**.

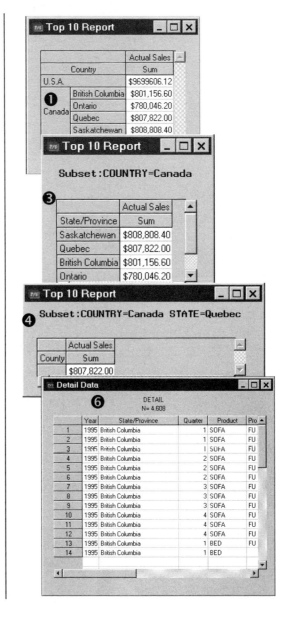

Creating a drillable tabular report

Change the report layout

To change the report layout, you can rotate the table and select the rows and columns to be displayed.

❶ Select **View ➤ Rotate**. Now the report displays a row for the sum of actual sales and countries as columns. Select **View ➤ Rotate** again to return the table to its original orientation.

❷ Select **View ➤ Report Layout** to open the *Column Selection* window. Notice that Down is selected by default under Type.

❸ In the Available list, double-click Product to move it to the Selected list.

❹ In the Type column, click Across.

❺ In the Available list, double-click Year to move it to the Selected list.

❻ Click OK. The chart now displays actual sales by year for each country and product.

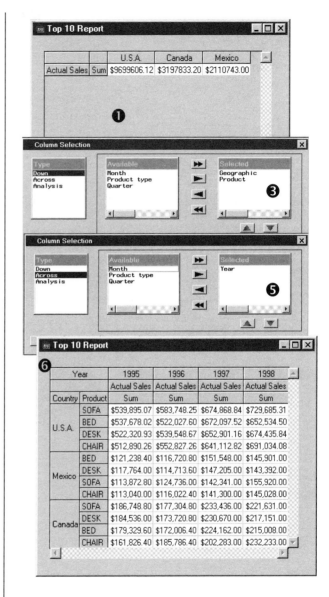

Subset by dimension

To restrict the data displayed in your report, you can subset by dimension.

❶ Select **View ➧ Subset by dimension**.

❷ For Dimension, select Quarter.

❸ In the Available list, double-click 1 to move it to the Selected list.

❹ Click OK. Now the report displays totals for only the first quarter, with the heading Subset: QUARTER=1.

❺ Select **View ➧ Clear Subset** to remove the subset.

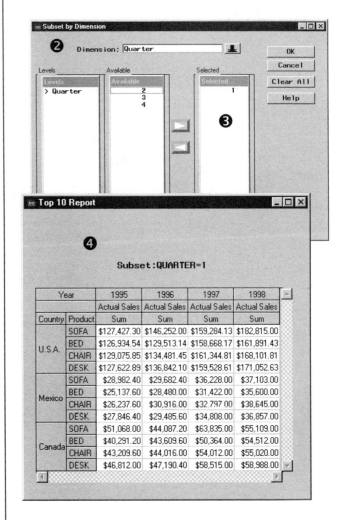

Calculate subtotals

In your report, you can calculate subtotals for rows, for columns, or for both.

1 To calculate subtotals for all products by country, right-click SOFA and select Computed Values from the pop-up menu.

2 Type `All Products` in the Description box.

3 Click the Calculation type drop-down arrow and select Sum of two or more values from the pop-up menu.

4 In the Values list, select SOFA, BED, CHAIR, and DESK. The formula for your calculation is displayed in the Formula box.

5 Click OK. The report now displays rows that subtotal sales for each country by year.

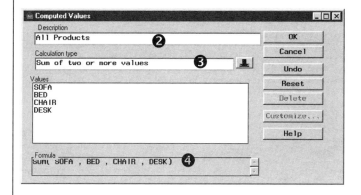

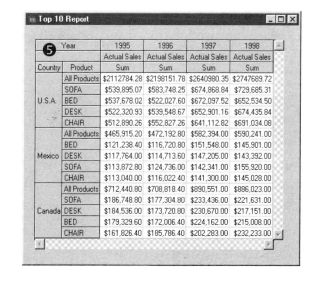

Save the report as a spreadsheet

You can save your report in a variety of formats, including Excel spreadsheets and SAS data sets.

① Select **File ➨ Save As**.

② Click the Excel spreadsheet tab. In the Label box, type My Excel File. Click the Save To arrow. Select a directory and type myexcel. Click Save or OK.

③ Click Create to create the new spreadsheet. Then click Close.

④ Select **File ➨ Close** to close the report.

⑤ From the *Gallery of Tabular Reports* window select **File ➨ Close**.

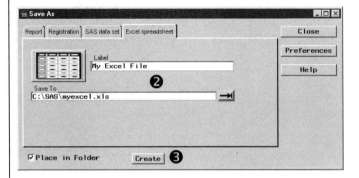

Creating a drillable graph

To quickly create interactive, drillable graphs, you can use report templates in the EIS / OLAP Report Gallery. This quick walkthrough shows you how to create and navigate a bar chart, change the graph type and report layout, and save the graph and the report definition.

To arrange icons in the window, you can right-click and select Line Up Items from the pop-up menu.

To create EIS / OLAP Report Gallery reports, you must first register the data you use. The following examples use the table Sashelp.Prdsal2, which has already been registered for your convenience. For details on registering your own data, see *Getting Started with SAS/EIS Software*.

Add a table

❶ Select **Solutions ➤ Reporting ➤ EIS / OLAP Report Gallery**.

❷ Double-click Graphical Reports and double-click Charts.

❸ In the *Gallery of Chart reports* window, open the pop-up menu and select Add Item. Then select Table to open the *Table Pointer Properties* window. Select SASHELP in the Library list and PRDSAL2 in the Table list. Click OK. The PRDSAL2 table icon appears in the *Gallery of Chart reports* window.

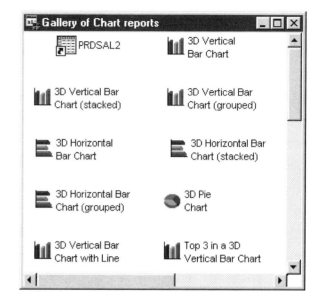

Creating a drillable graph

Create a basic graph

❶ Drag the PRDSAL2 table and drop it on 3D Vertical Bar Chart with Line. In the message dialog, click Yes.

❷ In the *Column Selection* window, Midpoint is selected by default under Type. In the Available list, double-click Geographic to move it to the Selected list.

❸ In the Type column, click Bar Variable. In the Available list, double-click Actual Sales to move it to the selected list.

❹ In the Type column, click Line Variable. In the Available list, double-click Predicted Sales to move it to the selected list.

❺ Click OK. The bar chart displays the sum of Actual Sales and the sum of Predicted Sales on the Y axis. The bars represent actual sales, and the line represents predicted sales. Country appears on the X axis.

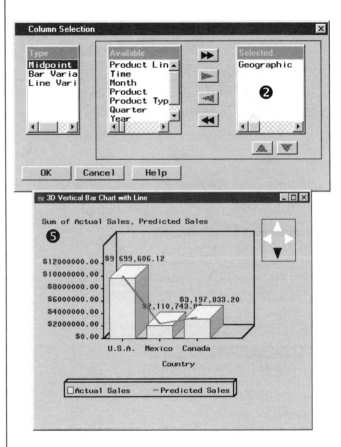

Format values

❶ Select **Tools ➡ Options ➡ Chart Options**. Click Formats.

❷ Actual Sales is selected by default. In the Format box, change DOLLAR12.2 to DOLLAR12.0. Then click Predicted Sales. In the Format box, change DOLLAR12.2 to DOLLAR12.0.

❸ Click OK. Dollar values in the chart now appear without decimal places.

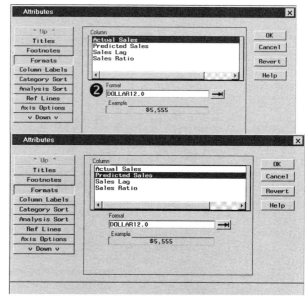

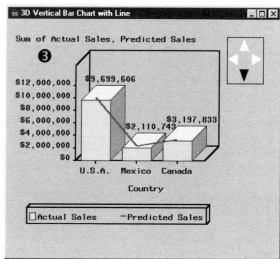

Creating a drillable graph

Navigate the chart

❶ To drill down in the chart, click the down arrow in the navigational arrows at the top of the chart. Now the chart displays State/Province on the X axis.

❷ To drill down further, click the down arrow again. Now the chart displays County on the X axis.

❸ To return to the original chart, click the up arrow twice.

❹ To view Canadian sales only, double-click the bar for Canada. Now the chart displays actual sales by region for Canada. To view only sales for the previous country in the chart, click the left arrow in the navigational arrows. Now the chart displays only actual sales by region for Mexico.

❺ Click the up arrow to return to the original chart.

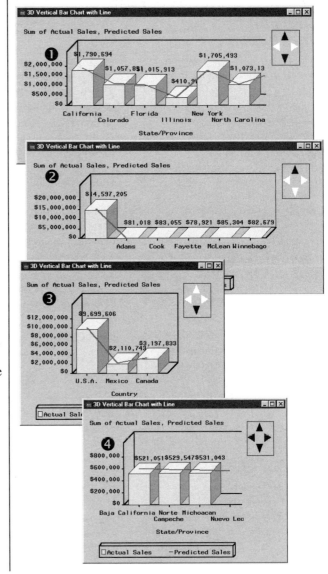

Creating a drillable graph

Change the graph type and report layout

❶ Select **View ➠ Change Chart Type**. In the Chart Type list, click 3D vertical bar (cylinder). Click OK. The chart is redisplayed with cylinders.

❷ Select **View ➠ Report Layout**. Notice that Midpoint is selected by default under Type. In the Selected list, double-click Geographic to remove it from the Selected list. In the Available list, double-click Product to move it to the Selected list.

❸ In the Type column, click Analysis. In the Selected list, double-click Actual Sales and Predicted Sales to move them out of the Selected list. Then double-click Sales Ratio to move it to the Selected List.

❹ Click OK. The chart now displays the sales ratio by product.

Tip

You can change the graph type and the layout of your chart at any time.

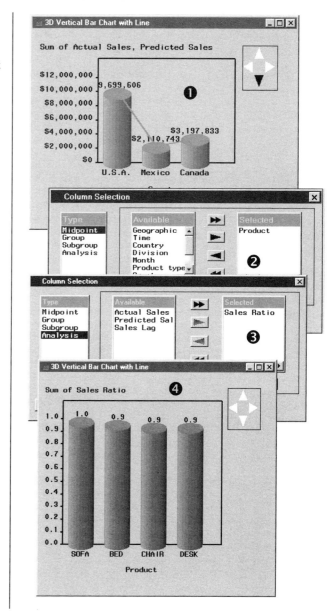

Creating a drillable graph

Note
When you create a graph that you want to reuse, you can save a snapshot of the graph or store its report definition. A report definition contains only instructions to produce the graph, not data or lines of output.

Save the graph
Save a snapshot of the graph.

❶ Select **File ➡ Snapshot**. Click the File Name arrow. In the Save As dialog, select a directory and type `barchart.gif`. Click Save or OK.

❷ Under Format in the *SAS/EIS Snapshot* window, click GIF. Under Orientation, click Landscape.

❸ Click Create. In the message dialog, click OK.

Save the report definition

❶ Select **File ➡ Save As**. In the label box, type `Revised Bar Chart`.

❷ Click Create. In the message dialog that appears, click OK. Then click Close.

❸ Select **File ➡ Close** to close the chart. Close both the *Gallery of Chart reports* and the *Gallery of Graphical reports* windows.

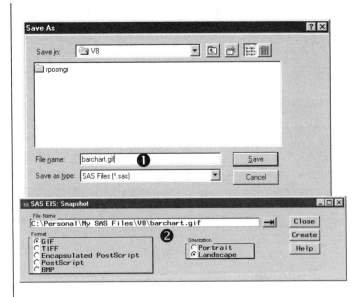

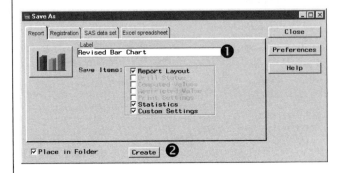

Creating a drillable multidimensional report

To create a drillable tabular report and drillable graph, you use a SAS table as input to reports. You can also use an MDDB (multidimensional database) to create reports. This quick walkthrough shows you how to create a basic report using an MDDB and save the report definition.

Note
To create EIS / OLAP Report Gallery reports, you must first register the data you use. The following examples use the table Sashelp.Prdsal2, which has already been registered for your convenience. For details on registering your own data, see *Getting Started with SAS/EIS Software*.

Add a table to use for reporting

For convenience, you can add an MDDB to your report gallery.

❶ Select **Solutions ➤ Reporting ➤ EIS / OLAP Report Gallery**.

❷ In the *Report Gallery folder* window, open the pop-up menu and select Add Item. Then select Multi-Dimensional Database.

❸ Click SASHELP in the Library list and PRDMDDB in the MDDB list.

❹ Click OK. The PRDMDDB table icon now appears in the *Report Gallery folder* window.

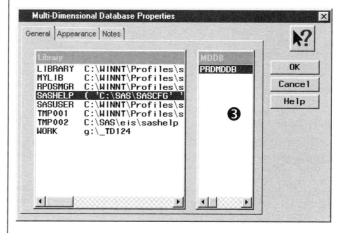

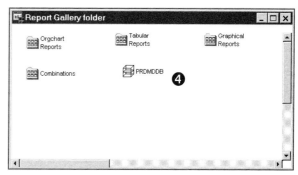

Create a basic table

To create a report, you can select from a list of reports appropriate to multidimensional databases.

❶ In the *Report Gallery folder* window, right-click the PRDMDDB table and select Report from the pop-up menu. Select Multi-dimensional Report. In the message window, click Yes.

❷ In the *Column Selection* window, Down Dimension is selected by default under Type. In the Available list, double-click Time.

❸ Under Type, click Across Dimension. In the Available list, double-click Geographic.

❹ Under Type, click Analysis Variables. In the Available list, double-click Sales Ratio.

❺ Click OK.

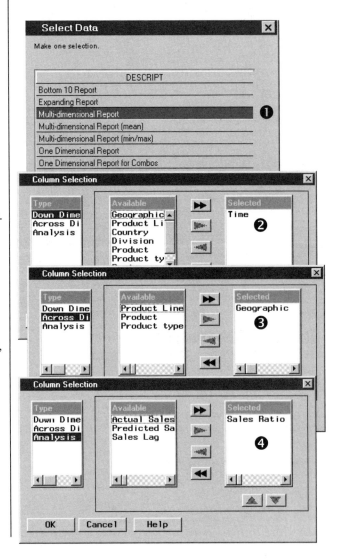

*Creating a drillable
multidimensional
report*

Change layout and statistics

❶ Select **View ➤ Rotate** to rotate the report layout. The report displays Year as columns and Country and Sales Ratio as rows.

❷ Select **View ➤ Change Statistic**. Select Sales Ratio and double-click Maximum, Minimum, and Percent of Sum in the Available list.

❸ Click OK. The report now displays the additional statistics you selected.

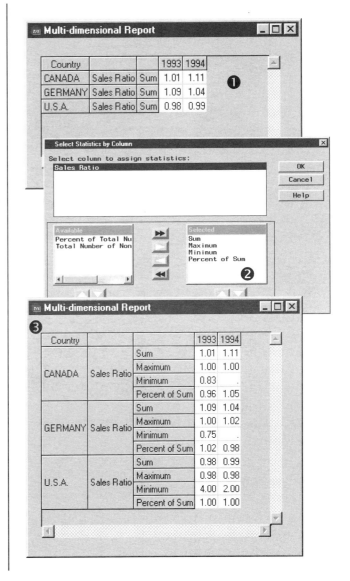

Save the report definition

You can store the definition for your report and use the definition to redisplay your report later with updated data.

❶ Select **File ➡ Save As**.

❷ In the Label box, type
Revised MD Report.

❸ Click Create.

❹ In the message window, click OK. Then click Close.

❹ Select **File ➡ Close** to close the report. Close the *Report Gallery Folder* window.

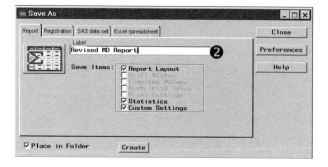

Notes

Notes

Chapter **5**

IN THIS SECTION

Starting a project in the Analyst Application

Creating summary statistics

Computing frequency counts

Performing a simple regression analysis

Creating a surface plot

Analyzing your data

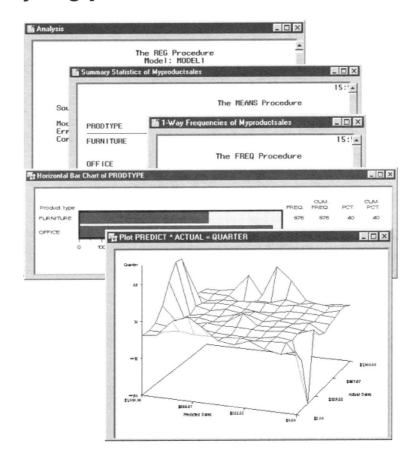

Starting a project in the Analyst Application

The Analyst Application provides easy access to commonly used statistical and graphical analysis capabilities. This quick walkthrough shows you how to start a project, select data, and set preferences. You can use this same project and data to do all the analyses in this chapter.

Start a project and open a table

❶ Select **Solutions ➡ Analysis ➡ Analyst**. A new project is created in the left pane of the *Analyst* window.

❷ Select **File ➡ Open By SAS Name**. Under Libraries, select Mylib. Then select Myproductsales. Click OK. The MyProductSales data appear in the table, and a node for the MyProductSales data is added to the tree under New Project.

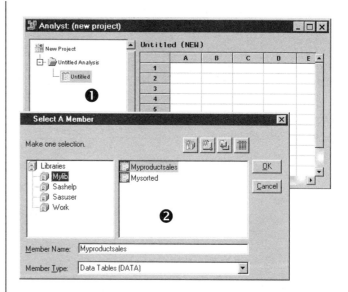

Set preferences

You can set a number of preferences for your project. In this example, you choose to display the programming code generated for each analysis.

❶ Select **Tools ➡ Viewer Settings**. Click the Output tab.

❷ Clear Create HTML file of results if it is selected. Select Provide source code. Then click OK.

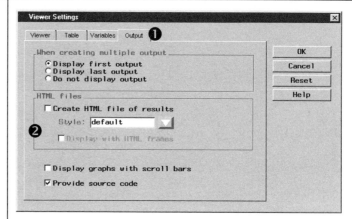

Creating summary statistics

To compute summary statistics, you can use the Analyst Application, which provides easy access to commonly used statistical and graphical analysis capabilities. This quick walkthrough shows you how to select variables and statistics, view and save your output.

Select a type of analysis, variables and statistics

For your analysis, you can specify class variables, analysis variables, and statistics.

❶ Select **Statistics → Descriptive → Summary Statistics**.

❷ Select ACTUAL. Then click Analysis.

❸ Select PREDICT. Then click Analysis.

❹ Select PRODTYPE. Then click Class.

❺ Click Statistics. In the *Summary Statistics: Statistics* window, make sure that Mean, Minimum, and Maximum are selected. Clear Standard deviation and Number of observations.

❻ Click OK.

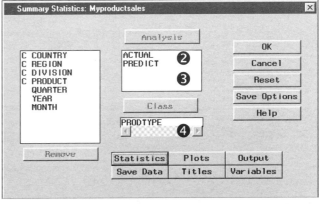

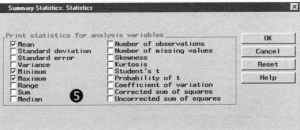

Creating summary statistics

View and save output

The results of your analysis are organized in a tree list in the *Analyst* window. You can save your results as a separate file, save them as an entry in a SAS catalog, or print them. In this example, you save results to a separate file.

❶ In the *Summary Statistics: Myproductsales* window, click OK to run your analysis. In the *Analyst* window, a Summary Statistics folder, containing Summary Statistics of Myproductsales and Code, is added to the project.

❷ View the output in the *Summary Statistics of Myproductsales* window.

❸ From the *Summary Statistics of Myproductsales* window, select **File ➡ Save As**.

❹ Type `summstat.lst` as the filename. Then click OK or Save.

❺ From the *Summary Statistics of Myproductsales* window, select **File ➡ Close.**

Tip
You can also save your entire project for later use.

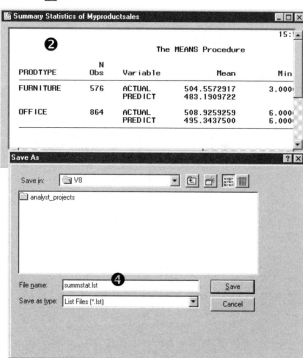

Computing frequency counts

To compute frequency counts, you can use the Analyst Application, which provides easy access to commonly used statistical and graphical analysis capabilities. This quick walkthrough shows you how to select statistics and view your output.

Select a type of analysis, variables, and statistics

For your frequency count analysis, you can specify variables, statistics and types of output (tables only, or tables and plots). In this example, you use the MyProductSales table you opened at the beginning of this chapter.

❶ Select **Statistics ➤ Descriptive ➤ Frequency Counts**. Double-click PRODTYPE to move it to the Frequencies box.

❷ Click Tables. Select Frequencies and percentages and click OK.

❸ Click Plots. Select Horizontal and click OK.

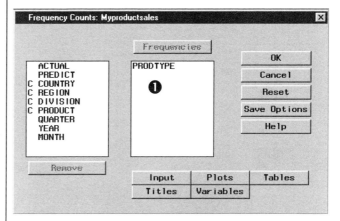

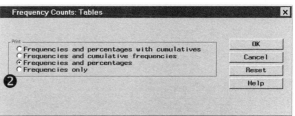

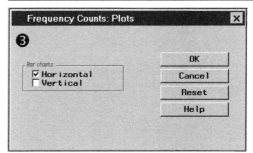

Run your analysis and view output

The results of your analysis are presented in separate windows and organized in a tree list in the *Analyst* window.

❶ In the *Frequency Counts: Myproductsales* window, click OK to run the analysis.

❷ View output in the *1-Way Frequencies of Myproductsales* window. Select **File ➡ Close**.

❸ In the *Analyst* window, notice that a Frequency Counts folder containing a Horizontal Bar Charts item has been added to the project. Double-click the Horizontal Bar Chart of PRODTYPE icon and view the graph. Then select **File ➡ Close**.

Tip

You can arrange the windows displaying the frequency table and the bar chart to view them simultaneously.

1-Way Frequencies of Myproductsales ▬ □ ✕

15:!

❷
The FREQ Procedure

Product type

PRODTYPE	Frequency	Percent
FURNITURE	576	40.00
OFFICE	864	60.00

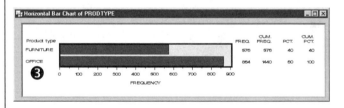

Horizontal Bar Chart of PRODTYPE

Product type		FREQ.	CUM. FREQ.	PCT.	CUM. PCT.
FURNITURE		576	576	40	40
OFFICE		864	1440	60	100

❸   0   100 200 300 400 500 600 700 800 900
FREQUENCY

Performing a simple regression analysis

The Analyst Application provides a wide range of analytical and graphical tasks such as computing descriptive statistics, performing simple hypothesis tests, and fitting models with analysis of variance and regression. This quick walkthrough shows you how to select a simple regression analysis, select variables and statistics, run your analysis, and view output.

Create and open sample data

For your analysis, you make a copy of the Houses table, which is sample data that the Analyst Application provides.

❶ Select **Tools ▸ Sample Data**. In the *Sample SAS data sets* window, select Houses. In the Create in box, leave the default Sasuser. Then click OK. The Houses data set is created in your Sasuser library.

❷ Select **File ▸ Open By SAS Name**. Under Libraries, select Sasuser. Then select Houses. Click OK.

❸ The Houses data appear in the table, and a folder for the Houses Analysis is added to the tree under New Project.

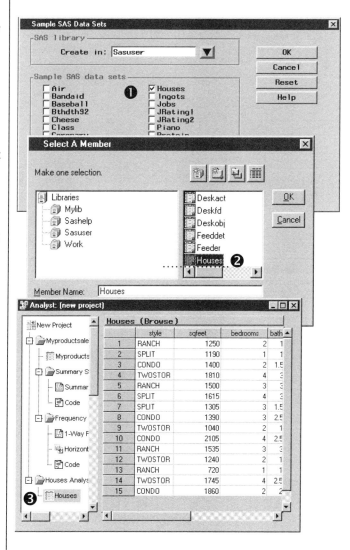

Performing a simple regression analysis

Select a type of analysis, variables, and statistics

For your analysis, you specify dependent and independent variables, the type of model, and statistics.

❶ Select **Statistics ➡ Regression ➡ Simple**.

❷ In the *Simple Linear Regression: Houses* window, select price. Then click Dependent.

❸ Select sqfeet. Then click Explanatory.

❹ Under Model, leave the default Linear selected.

❺ Click Statistics. Under Parameter estimates, select Confidence limits for estimates. Click OK.

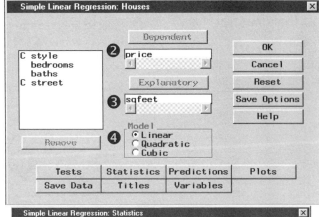

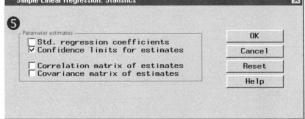

Tip

To select analyses, you can select **Statistics ➡ Index** and choose analyses from an index of tasks.

Run your analysis and view output

The results of your simple linear regression and the program code that created it are presented in separate windows and organized in a tree list in the *Analyst* window.

❶ In the *Simple Linear Regression: Houses* window, click OK to run the analysis.

❷ Scroll through output in the *Analysis* window. Select **File ➡ Close**.

Note
You can view program code for any analysis you run.

```
Analysis

                                The REG Procedure
❷                                 Model: MODEL1
                          Dependent Variable: price Asking price

                                Analysis of Variance

                                     Sum of          Mean
  Source               DF          Squares         Square     F Value    Pr > F

  Model                 1       7888892794     7888892794     3174.98    <.0001
  Error                13         32301206        2484708
  Corrected Total      14       7921194000


               Root MSE            1576.29571    R-Square     0.9959
               Dependent Mean         82720      Adj R-Sq     0.9956
               Coeff Var             1.90558


                                Parameter Estimates

                                     Parameter       Standard
  Variable    Label           DF      Estimate          Error    t Value    Pr > |t|

  Intercept   Intercept        1        -14982     1781.06635      -8.41     <.0001
  sqfeet      Square footage   1      67.52056        1.19830      56.35     <.0001
```

Creating a surface plot

Using the Analyst Application, you can easily produce graphs including histograms, box-and-whisker plots, probability plots, scatter plots, contour plots, and surface plots. This quick walkthrough shows you how to select a surface plot, select variables, view output, save the plot, and save the project as a whole.

Select a type of analysis and variables

For your surface plot, you specify variables for the *x*, *y*, and *z* axes. In this example, you use the MyProductSales table.

❶ Select **File ➜ Open By SAS Name**. Under Libraries, select Mylib. Then select Myproductsales. Click OK.

❷ Select **Graphs ➜ Surface Plot**.

❸ Select ACTUAL. Then click X Axis.

❹ Select PREDICT. Then click Y Axis.

❺ Select QUARTER. Then click Z Axis.

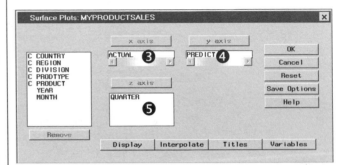

View and save the plot

Your surface plot is presented in a window and organized in a tree list in the *Analyst* window. You can save the plot.

❶ In the *Surface Plots: Myproductsales* window, click OK to perform the analysis. View the plot.

❷ From the *Plot PREDICT * ACTUAL = QUARTER* window, select **File ➡ Save As.**

❸ In the *Save As* window, type `surfplot.gif`. Be sure GIF file is selected as the file type. Click Save or OK.

❹ Select **File ➡ Close** to close the plot.

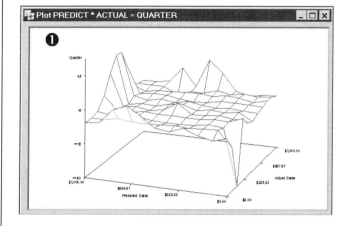

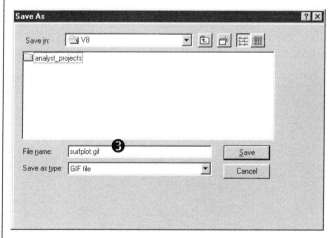

Save the project

You can save an entire project (including all the results and the tree list).

1 Select **File ➡ Projects ➡ Save**. The *Projects* window lists any existing projects.

2 In the Name box, type My Project. (For Path, leave the default value.)

3 Click OK. In the *Analyst* window, the project is now named My Project. The next time you start the Analyst Application, the saved project is opened automatically. If you have saved more than one project, you are prompted to open a saved project or begin a new project.

4 Select **File ➡ Close** to exit the Analyst Application.

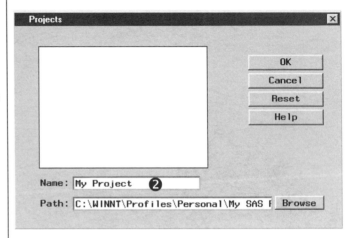

Chapter 6

Finding out more about SAS software

As you have worked through the tasks in this book, you have learned to use SAS software to accomplish basic data-driven tasks – data access and management, data analysis and data presentation. You can come back to these tasks any time you want to refresh your memory, or you can also try these tasks with your own data. Now that you are familiar with some of the tasks that you can do with SAS software, you may want to learn more about what SAS Institute has to offer.

SAS Institute's web site

On SAS Institute's web site (www.sas.com) you will find a wealth of information about SAS software products and applications, the latest news and events, and information about services available from SAS Institute.

Publications

Reference documentation for this release of SAS software is provided on CD-ROM. One copy is provided at no charge and additional copies may be purchased by contacting your local SAS office. The SAS OnlineDoc CD-ROM allows you to locate information you need quickly by using the table of contents or the full-text search facility. In addition to the CD-ROM, books are available in hardcopy form.

See the publications catalog for a complete listing of available documentation. The publications catalog is available in hardcopy form and on the SAS Publications web site (www.sas.com/pubs).

Training

SAS Institute offers a broad curriculum of instructor-based courses to help you use SAS software to meet your business goals. Courses cover a variety of general topics and many types of statistical analyses. Instructor-based training allows you the flexibility to attend courses in training facilities across the U.S. and in other countries. (Check with your local SAS office for availability.) In addition, Institute staff can conduct on-site training.

For descriptions of training courses, visit the SAS Training web site at www.sas.com/training.

SAS OnlineTutor is web-based interactive training that offers you an easy way to learn SAS programming skills right at your own desk. For more information, see www.sas.com/tutor.

Consulting

SAS Institute provides consulting services that enable your organization to get the most out of its investment in technology. Services include expertise on software, industry, and functional areas related to your immediate and future needs. Contact your local SAS office to get details on the SAS consulting services available in your area or visit the SAS Consulting web site at www.sas.com/consulting.

Technical Support

SAS Institute Technical Support provides a wide variety of services and resources to help you answer questions about SAS software. For detailed information about SAS Technical Support, see www.sas.com/ts.

For phone support in North America, call 919-677-8008 between 9:00 a.m. - 6:00 p.m. EST

In all other countries, call the Technical Support Division at your local SAS Institute office during office hours.

You can also send email to the Techical Support division at support@sas.com

Notes

Notes

Notes

Notes

Notes

Notes

Notes

Notes

Notes

Notes

Your Turn

If you have comments or suggestions about *Getting Started with the SAS® System, Version 8*, please send them to us on a photocopy of this page or send us electronic mail.

Send comments about this book to

SAS Institute Inc.
Publications Division
SAS Campus Drive
Cary, NC 27513
email: yourturn@sas.com

Send suggestions about the software to

SAS Institute Inc.
Technical Support Division
SAS Campus Drive
Cary, NC 27513
email: suggest@sas.com

*Welcome * Bienvenue * Willkommen * Yohkoso * Bienvenido*

SAS® Publications Is Easy to Reach

Visit our SAS Publications Web page located at www.sas.com/pubs

You will find product and service details, including

- **sample chapters**
- **tables of contents**
- **author biographies**
- **book reviews**

Learn about

- **regional user groups conferences**
- **trade show sites and dates**
- **authoring opportunities**
- **custom textbooks**

Order books with ease at our secured Web page!

Explore all the services that Publications has to offer!

Your Listserv Subscription Brings the News to You Automatically

Do you want to be among the first to learn about the latest books and services available from SAS Publications? Subscribe to our listserv **newdocnews-l** and automatically receive the following once each month: a description of the new titles, the applicable environments or operating systems, and the applicable SAS release(s). To subscribe:

1. Send an e-mail message to **listserv@vm.sas.com**

2. Leave the "Subject" line blank

3. Use the following text for your message:

> **subscribe newdocnews-l** *your-first-name your-last-name*

> For example: subscribe newdocnews-l John Doe

> **Please note:** newdocnews-l ◄───────── that's the letter "l" not the number "1".

For customers outside the U.S., contact your local SAS office for listserv information.

Create Customized Textbooks Quickly, Easily, and Affordably

SelecText® offers instructors at U.S. colleges and universities a way to create custom textbooks for courses that teach students how to use SAS software.

For more information, see our Web page at **www.sas.com/selectext**, or contact our SelecText coordinators by sending e-mail to **selectext@sas.com**.

You're Invited to Publish with SAS Institute's User Publishing Program

If you enjoy writing about SAS software and how to use it, the User Publishing Program at SAS Institute Inc. offers a variety of publishing options. We are actively recruiting authors to publish books, articles, and sample code. Do you find the idea of writing a book or an article by yourself a little intimidating? Consider writing with a co-author. Keep in mind that you will receive complete editorial and publishing support, access to our users, technical advice and assistance, and competitive royalties. Please contact us for an author packet. E-mail us at **sasbbu@sas.com** or call 919-677-8000, then press 1-6479. See the SAS Publications Web page at **www.sas.com/pubs** for complete information.

Read All about It in *Authorline*®!

Our User Publishing newsletter, *Authorline*, features author interviews, conference news, and informational updates and highlights from our User Publishing Program. Published quarterly, *Authorline* is available free of charge. To subscribe, send e-mail to **sasbbu@sas.com** or call 919-677-8000, then press 1-6479.

See *Observations*®, Our Online Technical Journal

Feature articles from *Observations*®: *The Technical Journal for SAS*® *Software Users* are now available online at **www.sas.com/obs**. Take a look at what your fellow SAS software users and SAS Institute experts have to tell you. You may decide that you, too, have information to share. If you are interested in writing for *Observations*, send e-mail to **sasbbu@sas.com** or call 919-677-8000, then press 1-6479.

Book Discount Offered at SAS Public Training Courses!

When you attend one of our SAS Public Training Courses at any of our regional Training Centers in the U.S., you will receive a 15% discount on any book orders placed during the course. Each course has a list of recommended books to choose from, and the books are displayed for you to see. Take advantage of this offer at the next course you attend!

SAS Institute Inc.
SAS Campus Drive
Cary, NC 27513-2414
Fax 919-677-4444

E-mail: sasbook@sas.com
Web page: www.sas.com/pubs
To order books, call Fulfillment Services at 800-727-3228*
For other SAS Institute business, call 919-677-8000*

* Note: Customers outside the U.S. should contact their local SAS office.